To my Grandma,

who saw the release of the first and second edition of this book before she passed. I will always love and miss you.

TABLE OF CONTENTS

Introduction

Religion not included. Meditation is for everyone.

When you think of meditation, you probably imagine some orange robed monk or spiritual guru with a beard or bald head, sitting cross-legged with his eyes closed. You probably think of Buddhism or spirituality.

If you're like most westerners, you're not a Buddhist, and therefore may have some objections:

- "Catholics don't meditate!"
- "Why would an atheist or agnostic meditate?"
- "Are Muslims even allowed to meditate?"

The truth is you don't need to be Buddhist, religious, or even spiritual in order to meditate. You can just be a normal dude or dudette with a busy life, who's looking to bring some calmness, peace, and clarity into it.

Whatever your background, meditation can be a practical tool to improve the quality or your life. It can help you with decision-making, emotional stability, problem-solving and so much more.

What will your friends and family think of you?

Some of you may be embarrassed to meditate. You may wonder what people will think of you - like you're some new age hippy who's trying to change the world.

First off, you don't need to tell anyone you meditate. Meditation can be as public or private as you want it to be. The choice to tell others about it is entirely up to you.

If you do make it known to your family, friends or whoever, you'll help pave the way for meditation to move into the mainstream, and help break its association with religion. You'll be walking proof that ordinary dudes and dudettes can meditate. Not to be spiritual, not to change the world, but only to change yourself.

What will you learn about in this book?

I'm gonna teach you how to meditate – straight up, without the religion, fluff, or hippy stuff. I'm also gonna teach you:

- A simple, easy-to-understand definition of meditation
- How meditation can benefit you
- A bit about my personal history with meditation
- Some common ways people meditate – chanting, thought repetition, etc.
- Some ideas on how to integrate meditation into your daily life

I'll also answer some common questions about meditation. But before we get started, I want to show you just how common meditating actually is.

People in the spotlight who meditate

While the following list of people may not be ordinary in every sense of the word - they're celebrities - here are some famous folks who meditate once or twice a day.

Jake Gyllenhaal
Actor

Sheryl Crow

Musician

Donovan
Singer and Songwriter

Mike Love
Singer from the Beach Boys

Paul McCartney
The Beatles

Ringo Starr
The Beatles

Katy Perry
Musician

Jennifer Aniston
Actress

Russell Brand
Actor

Jeff Bridges
Actor

Oprah Winfrey
Producer and Talk Show Host

David Lynch
Director

Clint Eastwood
Actor and Director

Gisele Bündchen
Fashion model

Joaquim Chissano
Former president of Mozambique

Cameron Diaz
Actress

Hugh Jackman
Actor

Phil Jackson
NBA executive

Pau Gasol
NBA player

Gretchen Bleiler
Snowboarder

Chapter 1

How meditation helped me beat anxiety

Okay, so I'm just gonna say it – when I first started meditation at the wide-eyed and bushy-tailed age of 19, I was a bit of a new-age hippy, obsessed with philosophy, spirituality and the exploration of religions. This book is not about that, but I still feel it's important for me to share how I got to where I am today with my meditation practice: a state where it has nothing to do with religion, spirituality, or changing the world.

The intention behind my meditation practice is simple – to change myself so I can have a better life, a clear mind, and an increased feeling of calm. If I do that, I can be my best self - every day of my life. And in the process I'll be able to treat the people I care about with more respect, patience and kindness.

Over a decade of practice, meditation has helped me do just that. It has served as a consistent guidepost in my life, and has brought me more happiness and calm than I could have ever imagined when I first started at 19. By reading this book, I hope you can let it do the same for you.

So this is how it all began...

At 19, I had a pretty serious anxiety problem. I felt nervous all the time and even suffered panic attacks. Like most teenagers, I simply wanted to feel normal. And anxiety got in the way of that, causing social awkwardness and difficulty talking to girls. So I figured the best way to fix this problem was through reading. And at that time, it made sense that maybe some exotic religion had the answer. So I started exploring...

I read books on Hinduism, surfed the web for info about Islam, got lost in the aisles of the Spirituality section at Barnes & Noble, and read everything I could about Buddhism. It was through Buddhism that I first discovered meditation.

After about nine months of endless reading, it occurred to me that I had to try something else besides absorbing information. This is when I decided to give meditation a go. From everything I read, it seemed proven to help calm an anxious mind.

So that summer, between working at McDonald's and reading on my parents' back porch while basking in the summer sunshine, I started taking 30-minute breaks to sit on a beat-up, gray folding chair in my old bedroom, and do what I imagined was meditation. Some days I would simply sit on the chair and pay attention to my breathing, other times I would repeat a phrase over and over again in my mind, and some days I would just stare at a spot on the floor.

As summer drew to a close, I returned to college...

The coming semester, I continued my meditation practice and enrolled in an extracurricular meditation course being offered at the University Rec Center. Over the six-week class, we learned different types of meditation, including listening to music and instruments, as well as walking meditation and chanting.

The main thing I took away from that six-week period was that I wanted to keep meditating. And from then on, I was hooked. I started meditating every day - most of the time sitting on my bed, with my back up against the wall, and paying attention to my breathing while staring at a spot on my blanket. As months passed, my meditation sessions increased from 30 minutes to an hour - and some days even an hour and a half (I know, I was obsessed!)

The most important thing to me was the payoff. I was reaping the benefits of meditation: feeling calmer and more centered. And as time passed, my anxiety problems became less severe. By the time I was 22, I no longer had any anxiety issues at all.

With anxiety no longer a problem, my meditation practice nearly fizzled out. I didn't return to a daily meditation practice until I was 30. And since starting again it has once again had an amazingly transformational effect on my life. Not only has it dramatically improved my personal relationships, but it has also helped me find direction in my career path, become calmer, and see the bigger picture when life has become stressful.

So, what's the secret to meditation's transformational power? And how can it personally help you? Let's take a closer look....

Chapter 2

How meditation transforms you

In this chapter, we're gonna take a closer look at meditation, and how it changes the way you experience everyday life. To start off, let's look at what meditation is in its simplest form. Here's an easy definition.

To meditate is to withdraw attention from thought

As you'll read later in this book, all forms of meditation have one thing in common - they all focus on withdrawing attention from thought. Now, to be exceedingly clear, there is nothing wrong with thinking in and of itself, and the goal of meditation isn't to completely stop thoughts - that's impossible. Instead, you're shifting your attention away from thought to something that is happening right now (like your breathing, sounds you hear, the feelings you experience in your body, etc.). The easiest way I've discovered to do this is through stillness.

The simplest way to meditate is to be still

During meditation, focus on the stillness of your body - not on mental activity. For example, if a thought comes up like "what am I going to have for dinner tonight?", don't answer the question or even think about it. Instead, ignore it and simply pay attention to the stillness of your body.

By doing this you're withdrawing attention from mental activity and, when this happens, a space is created between your thoughts. Now you are fully aware of what's going on in your head.

Fully aware? And that means what?

When you hear the word "aware", what does that mean to you?

Personally, when I started reading meditation books and the monk authors started dropping the word "aware" on me, I was always scratching my head, a bit confused as to what they were actually talking about. Sure, to "be aware" means to simply know something exists. But what does this have to do with meditation? And why is it so important?

The thing about awareness is that it's easy to take for granted. Every single moment of our day we're aware at all times - whether we like it or not. In fact, if you stop reading right now, you can easily be aware of dozens of different things around you...

So stop, take a moment and ask yourself:

- What do you hear?
- What do you see?
- Where are you?
- What do you smell?
- What do you feel?

If you take the time, you can probably come up with a hundred different answers to these questions. But the real question is, how does this apply to meditation? Let's take a closer look...

Say you live on a busy street. There's lots of noise and racket going on outside almost all the time, but during the day you may not even notice it. Maybe this is because you're watching TV, chatting with friends, cleaning your house, or doing something else. Whatever you're doing, you're so focused on what's going on indoors that you aren't aware of the noise outside.

So what happens when you slow down? Maybe you decide to plop down on your couch, and just lay back and relax – without any music, TV or other noise to distract you. Suddenly, you're completely aware of all the noises outside. You hear the dog bark, the cars honking their horns, and your loud neighbors bickering. Now that you've slowed down, you are **fully aware** of the outside noise.

A similar thing happens in your daily life with thoughts. During your day, you may be too busy to be aware of any of the racket (aka your thoughts) going on in your head. When you stop, slow down and meditate, all of a sudden you notice a whole world of mental activity you may never have known existed.

Becoming more aware of what's going on around you, both in and outside your body, is the secret to meditation's transformational power. As a newcomer to meditation, one of the first things you'll notice in your initial month of practice is just how often you're actually thinking. And as you become more aware of this, eventually you'll naturally start to create space between your thoughts.

Space between thoughts?

Okay, you may be a bit perplexed by what "space between thoughts" means. But it really is exactly what it sounds like: a space or gap between two thoughts. Many people live their lives thinking non-stop, so an actual space between thoughts may rarely, if ever, happen. Because of this, the idea can be a bit hard to grasp. So to give you a clearer idea of this concept and how it can impact you, let's look at the following metaphor.

Imagine you're having a TV series marathon: you're spending your afternoon plopped down on the couch watching episode after episode of your favorite show. As you watch, the story on the screen sends you on an emotional rollercoaster. You laugh with the characters, grow anxious when they do, and even experience the sadness they feel. Now, after a couple hours into the marathon, you've come to the emotional climax of the story. Your heart sinks, your face begins to flush, and your eyes well up with tears. You can't help but feel the heartache the character is experiencing, and tears begin to stream down your face...

Then, all of a sudden, the power cuts out and the TV turns off. Suddenly you become aware that you're now sitting in a dark room with a blank television screen in front of you. And to your surprise, you realize you'd been so wrapped up in the TV series that you were crying. As you wipe the tears off your cheek in disbelief, you laugh to yourself, amused that you were so moved by the images you were watching.

Then, before you know it, the power returns and the TV series continues to play. You return your attention to the story and characters.

This metaphor demonstrates the impact that space between thoughts can have. Essentially, all your thoughts are like the story that plays on the TV screen. The power outage is the space between them. As you saw in the metaphor, this space can create a temporary detachment from the stream of thoughts. Not only does it put them in perspective, but it also brings calmness, emotional stability, and common sense to your situation. Over months of consistent meditation practice, these gaps of space will become more and more common for you.

The role of "space between thoughts" in meditation

Creation of space between thoughts is an integral part of what makes meditation so effective. Essentially, the space slows down your thought process and creates moments of no thinking.

Try it right now and see if you can create some space. Become very still, and just pay attention to the thoughts passing through your brain. What happens?

Seriously, don't skip to the next page until you try this. It will only take a minute...

Welcome back. So, maybe it was just for a moment, but you likely noticed that your thoughts either stopped completely or suddenly slowed down. In a sense, this exercise is like stepping on the brakes of your thought process, which is the same thing that happens when you meditate. And the space created by doing this plays a key role in how you react to a given situation.

With space comes a choice

Let's return to the metaphor of the house on the busy street. We left off with you lying on the couch relaxing…

As you lie still, you hear your neighbors bickering loudly again. Now that you're completely aware of this, you realize you have a choice as to how to respond. You can choose how to act.

For one, maybe you can just put some background noise on to drown out their voices. Two, maybe you decide to go over to their house, explain your situation, and politely ask them to be quiet. Another option, well, you could also just call the police. Not the nicest thing to do, but certainly an option. Whatever you choose to do, the point is that with awareness come options and choices.

In meditation, choose stillness

While you meditate, your sole task is to create these pockets of space in between your thoughts. Now, you might be overwhelmed as to how you actually do this. As already mentioned, though, it's quite simple - just be still. Whenever a thought distracts you, bring your attention back to your body, back to your stillness.

By being still, you're automatically slowing down the thought process, and the gaps will come naturally. Within this space is not only choice, but also peace. When you meditate, you give yourself the opportunity to choose peace. Without this space, you likely never even knew you had a choice.

The space created during meditation will eventually appear in your everyday life

Meditation is a lot like exercise for your brain. When you start exercising at the gym, you don't see the results immediately. In fact, you likely don't even notice a difference till a month or two later. But maybe one day, after you've been exercising on a regular basis, one of your co-workers mentions how much stronger and leaner you look. Or maybe you wake up one morning and realize you have a lot more energy than you used to.

Just like exercise impacts every aspect of your daily life - from how you feel to your physical appearance - so does meditation. With practice, you'll not only feel less stressed throughout your day, but you'll also appear more calm and at ease. Space between thoughts is also a result of regular practice. And here's how it can impact you...

Imagine it's an ordinary day and you're stuck in traffic after work. You start to feel irritated and you notice yourself becoming angry.

Maybe you start to think, "Why is there traffic now? This road is always empty! These idiots don't know how to drive! How am I ever going to make it to my dinner date in time?"

Ordinarily, in a situation like this, your anger may continue to build and stay with you for the rest of the day. But with increased meditation practice, you'll remember you have a choice. You can choose not to be angry. So instead of following the chain of negative thoughts, return your attention back to your body, and become as still as you can (of course without causing yourself to get into a car accident.)

It's important to note that the anger is not going to disappear instantly, but instead slowly begin to dissipate, eventually going away on its own.

When you stop tossing logs in the fire, the flames still burn

Because thoughts are continually passing through your consciousness on a daily basis, they have a momentum that takes time to slow down. To demonstrate how this works, let's look at another metaphor.

At one point or another, you've likely sat around a campfire. Maybe you were off in the middle of the woods somewhere with friends, on the beach at night, or in your backyard. Regardless of your location, the same basics of campfire fundamentals always apply: when you continuously throw logs in the fire, it continues to burn brightly.

Now, what happens when you suddenly stop tossing logs in? The fire keeps burning, right? But what happens if no wood is fed into the flames for a minute, then five minutes, then an hour? Obviously, the fire starts to go out.

The thought process works the same thought is a log that fuels more thinking, activity. You keep the fire burning with y(attention to it - your constant attenti thoughts.

When you take that attention away, and bring it back to your body and stillness, you stop tossing more logs in. Negative thoughts and feelings then slowly begin to extinguish themselves. Eventually they'll be replaced with increased calm.

Chapter 3

Quick rundown of benefits

Thus far, we've briefly gone over a few of the benefits of meditation. In this chapter, we're going to explore some of these benefits in a bit more depth, to show you how meditation can dramatically improve your life.

1. Increased calm

This is one of the biggest benefits of consistent meditation practice. And to explain how it does this, I'm going to use a few ideas from the last chapter.

Basically, the main way meditation increases calmness is by decreasing reactivity. Many people are stuck in a continual cycle of reaction, and the campfire metaphor is a perfect example of this. The normal person is thinking all the time. Logs are continually thrown into the fire of their consciousness day in and day out. And because of this, they simply react to the situations they encounter every day with little choice in the matter.

Essentially, your thoughts are like a car speeding down the highway with no brakes. If you're a passenger in this car, you notice houses, scenery and animals as they pass by. You'd like to stop or maybe change direction, but you can't because you're caught up in the momentum. Sounds a bit nerve wracking to be in this car, right? I mean, you have no brakes!

It can be just as nerve wracking when uncontrolled thoughts are racing through your mind on a daily basis, and you have no idea how to make them stop.

Meditation gives you your brakes back. Actually, your brakes have been there all along, but when you meditate you simply remember they're there. And now that you're aware of them, you realize you don't actually need to stop your thoughts, but simply put them in perspective. They are just thoughts, and they can't harm you. But when you're able to slow down the mental activity, it becomes easier to see this. You can enjoy the ride, change direction, stop off for an ice cream, whatever.

So, what does it feel like to experience decreased reactivity?

It all comes down to choice. Meditation brings choice into your life, where you didn't even realize you had one before. And since we're on the topic of cars and highways, let's just keep with this theme for the following example...

Say you're driving down the highway and someone cuts you off. Let's say you're normally the type of person who has a bit of road rage, and you instantly lay on your horn, give this asshole the finger, and scream, "F%#$#* you, hillbilly!" You likely become really pissed off and may even decide to tailgate this jerk. Whether or not you do, you remain irritated for the next couple hours because of this one singular event.

Now let's say this same event happens to you after you've been meditating consistently for a few months. When this guy cuts you off, instead of automatically laying on the horn, whipping out the finger, and screaming at him, you're instead aware of this reaction as a physical impulse before actually enacting it. Instead of the words "F%#$#* you, hillbilly!" automatically spewing from your lips, you're aware of them as a thought in your head first. With this awareness, you now have a choice. You can choose to yell out these words, shoot him the finger - and be irritated for hours. Or you can choose to let it go.

With this choice, what would you rather do? Would you rather be angry for hours? Or would you rather let it go, remain calm, and pleasantly go about your day? This is the power of meditation. This is how it decreases your reactivity, replaces it with a choice, and gives you an ocean of calmness along the way.

2. Clearer mind

As mentioned in the last chapter, when you meditate you gain more space in your mind. And when there's more space in your mind, you naturally gain more clarity. Here's an example to demonstrate how it works.

Imagine there is a pond outside your house...

On a rainy day, you watch the pond from the window of your bedroom on the second floor. It's impossible to see anything under the surface of the water. When the rain turns into a drizzle, you go outside, and now you can start to see some of the fish swimming under the surface of the water.

The next day, it's sunny and clear outside. You go back to the pond and, this time with no rain obstructing the view from the surface, you can see all the way to the bottom of the pond - the fish, seaweed, everything.

Each drop of rain on the pond's surface is like a thought in your mind. When there are lots of thoughts, like on a rainy day, it's impossible to think clearly. Everything is coming so fast and so hard, one thing after another, that you can't notice anything but the thoughts. You get caught up in them, and can't see the clarity that exists just below the surface.

When you meditate, the heavy rains will begin to subside. With enough practice, they'll eventually become a drizzle.

Will it ever be a sunny day?

The goal of meditation is not to get rid of thoughts. Thoughts are a part of being human, and even meditation masters (who may not be very ordinary dudes) don't have a completely clear mind. But in their minds, it's never pouring. And it's likely even less than a drizzle.

3. Ability to problem-solve and remember better

So you're meditating, reacting less, and suddenly you're seeing the spaces between your thoughts. You're not getting so involved with all the nonsense in your head, and daily headaches are becoming less irritating.

The traffic on your commute to work is suddenly no big deal. That person at work who always gets under your skin becomes less of an annoyance. And even your partner's complaints about your bad habits (you know you have 'em) seem to bother you less. Now there's this extra space to fill.

The extraordinary thing that happens is that within this space you start to remember things you'd forgotten about - things that were buried under all the busyness at the surface.

To give you an example of how meditation can improve your memory, let's return to the pond and rain metaphor. Let's say a few months ago you were swimming in the pond when your watch fell off your wrist. You were having so much fun splashing around in the water that you didn't even notice it was missing till weeks later. Now that you know it's gone...if you go search for your watch outside in the pouring rain, are you going to find it? Even if you look in the pond, you'd never spot it because it would be impossible to see under the surface of the water. But when the rain slows down, you might look in the pond again and suddenly find your lost watch.

Just like with the rain in the pond, too much thinking makes it hard to see past the surface. Instead of remembering things, like the birthday of a friend or family member, or an important task you need to take care of, you may be caught up with thoughts about your day, the hillbilly who cut you off on your drive home from work, or what's on TV tonight. Meditation allows you to see past all this, look deeper below the surface, and remember forgotten things.

How do you solve problems?

To understand how meditation helps with problem solving, let's examine a core issue that causes problems to fester, as well as a common tactic used to overcome this: temporarily walking away. Take a look at your own experience. Has there ever been a time when you were trying to solve a problem and couldn't find an answer?

You pushed and pushed and pushed to the point that it felt like you were slamming your head against the wall. Then, you finally decided to walk away from the problem…

Hours passed and you completely forgot about it. Then maybe the next day or in the evening, out of nowhere, the answer appears. Has this happened to you?

I've resolved countless problems by temporarily walking away from them. But perhaps the most memorable time occurred when I was backpacking in Australia.

I had just gotten to Oz from a four-month trip in Asia, and was down to my last $900 and desperately looking for a job. I'd spent a few weeks searching non-stop, and I was extremely stressed out as I didn't want to end up on the streets in a foreign country. So I decided to stop, slow down, and walk away from the problem for a few days. I took that time to relax and get back to the reason I started traveling in the first place: to experience a new country.

So I did touristy things, like visiting a popular market and knocking back some beers with people in my hostel. During this break, a few things happened that still surprise me to this day. First, I realized that I hated where I was staying in Melbourne.

Basically it was in the very busy concrete jungle of the Central Business District (CBD). So I decided to get the hell out of there and head for a hostel located on one of the beaches in the suburbs. But before I did, I ended up making some new friends at the hostel in the CBD.

That's when I met a German fellow named Bjorn who tipped me off to exactly what I was looking for – a high-paying job in the countryside. He gave me the contact details of a woman who had helped him there and, before I knew it, I had a new job out in the sticks and was pulling in over a thousand dollars a week.

The point is that when I walked away from the problem and took some time to relax, the resolution came almost naturally.

While this example describes a more unusual situation, taking some time away from a problem can also help with more common issues that almost all of us encounter. It doesn't matter whether you're trying to decide if you should accept a new job, or simply trying to find where you put the TV remote - you may be surprised how easily answers appear when you walk away and relax.

What causes a problem to fester?

Walking away from a problem essentially diffuses any overwhelming emotions you may be experiencing - such as panic, frustration, or irritation. This brings us to one of the core reasons that causes a problem to amplify: overwhelming emotions.

Overwhelming emotion is a breeding ground for bad decisions. In the example above, when I was short on cash in Australia, I was overwhelmed with the fear and anxiety that I could end up on the streets. And if I didn't walk away from the situation and clear my head, this very well could have turned into a reality.

While that story involves serious consequences, overwhelming emotions can also prevent effective problem-solving in more everyday situations.

Let's face it, many of us get wound up over small, insignificant issues. For example, maybe you're trying to troubleshoot a problem you're experiencing with your computer. If you become overwhelmed with frustration, how likely are you to resolve your issue? Probably not very well, if at all.

If you instead walk away from the issue, you essentially diffuse the frustration, panic or other strong emotion you may be feeling. After you relax, you can come back to the problem, look at it with a clear head, and solve it in a more rational manner.

What does "walking away from a problem" have to do with meditation?

When you walk away from a problem, it becomes much easier to notice when your thinking is clouded with overwhelming emotion. And regular meditation does the exact same thing.

When you meditate, you're much less likely to get wound up, overwhelmed, or frustrated over little problems in the first place. Instead, you'll be more relaxed and more emotionally stable on a regular basis, and because of this it will be easier for problems to resolve themselves naturally.

Meditation also enhances creativity

So maybe you're an artist of some sort. Maybe you like to write, paint, tell stories, shoot videos, design living spaces or what not.

Along with the new problem-solving skills and better memory your mind gains from meditation, you also get a sudden boost of creativity. Just like a relaxed mind is better at solving problems, it's better at creating and coming up with ideas too. The key word here is "relax".

Think about it, when you're relaxed, isn't life easier? The same goes for creativity. Ideas will present themselves more easily, and your mind will put up less resistance to your creative flow.

4. Better sense of direction

A calm mind is the source of meditation's transformative power on the everyday, ordinary dude or dudette. Better problem-solving skills, more creativity, and more patience are the direct result of this enhanced calm. And this is also true for gaining a better sense of direction. To demonstrate this, let's look at another metaphor.

Imagine you're driving to meet some friends at a bar in an unfamiliar city. The only directions you have are handwritten on a piece of paper. It's easy to follow them at first, but then it starts snowing.

Suddenly visibility is becoming difficult. It's hard to see the road signs. Even worse, there's no one around to ask for directions. The streets have turned into a ghost town, and businesses have shut down because they heard about the storm in advance. You unfortunately did not.

Similar to the rain in a previous metaphor, the snow is just like your thoughts. When thoughts are racing through your mind, it can be difficult to see the right direction to take. It's difficult to see where to go, obstacles to avoid, and where the signposts are that can point you in the right direction.

Also, notice how the people who would have been available to help you have disappeared because of the heavy snowfall. When your thoughts are racing, you'll be less likely to notice that there are others around you ready to lend you a helping hand.

People use the term "lost in thought" for a reason. Meditation snaps you out of the endless stream of thoughts and makes it easier to see the signposts that take you where you want to go.

Chapter 4

How others meditate

People have been meditating for centuries. And over this time, various forms of it have developed. Let's take a look at four common variations of meditation still in practice today.

1. Chanting

Ommmmmm...oooommmmmmmm.

In other words, chanting. If in the future you ever go to a Buddhist temple or do group meditation, you may encounter this meditation practice.

Personally, I've participated in chanting meditation very few times. And the last time was in a meditation class nearly a decade ago.

Why people chant

The purpose of chanting is to withdraw your attention from normal everyday thoughts, and instead focus on the group chant. It's similar to how you shift your attention when you're at a movie theatre.

When you enter the theatre, maybe you're busy thinking about what you'll eat for dinner, plans for the weekend, or some new car or piece of furniture you want. Once the movie starts, within minutes all those thoughts disappear and you focus instead on the actors, actresses and story playing out on the screen.

In chanting, you're essentially doing the same thing.

The difference is that you're focusing on the group chant instead of a movie. And like a movie, it can truly be hypnotic and a well-needed vacation from a busy brain.

A quick word on the use of tone in chanting

Sounds and tone of voice oftentimes contain an emotional aspect that can have a dramatic effect on how we feel: a powerful speech can move us to tears, the sound of laughter can make us smile (even if we're not in on the joke), and hearing someone criticize another can make us feel irritated.

When it comes to chanting, every chant I've ever heard or participated in has had one thing in common: it has been spoken and repeated by all participants in a monotone.

Unlike the wide variety of tones we hear every day in conversations with coworkers, friends and others, the monotone you speak and hear in a group chant lacks any emotion; and therefore it will not cause your mood to fluctuate.

Instead, the monotone can have a calming effect on us, much like the sound of steady rain on your windowsill or the white noise from a fan in your home.

Nowadays, I still encounter chanting meditation when I join my girlfriend and her family at their Buddhist temple. I always ignore it and instead focus on my own simple meditation, which I'll get to in the next chapter.

2. Thought repetition - mantras

Back in my early days of meditation, I used to experiment with thought repetition. I have more experience with this than chanting, but not by much.

Basically, it involves repeating the same thoughts over and over again in your mind while you are sitting still in meditation.

If you've never heard of thought repetition, perhaps a more common name for this is repeating a mantra. It's been a very long time since I've done this type of meditation but, from what I recall, a mantra I used to repeat when I practiced went something like this:

I am one with the world
I am one with my breath
I am one with all of life and the universe

Something like that...usually the idea is that a mantra should be some kind of uplifting sentence, or group of sentences, that makes you feel good.

However, some people also like to repeat mantras in foreign languages.

Lokah Samastah Sukhino Bhavantu

Om Gum Ganapatayei Namah

These two mantras are both in Sanskrit. Now, why would people choose to repeat a mantra in a language other than their own?

Well, whether or not you understand the words you're repeating, all mantras have a similar purpose: you withdraw attention from your thoughts.

Additionally, many non-English mantras come from India (including the ones above) and were created thousands of years ago. They were written in a specific way where the phonetics are supposed to have a positive effect on your psyche, and help you reach a meditative state more easily.

How do you practice thought repetition?

It's quite easy. You literally just repeat a mantra over and over again for your entire meditation – whether that's five minutes or an hour.

Like chanting meditation, it's supposed to focus your brain so that your mind is less distracted by thoughts. The difference is that chanting is generally more group-based, whereas thought repetition is often performed by solo practitioners.

With that said, oftentimes a person repeating a mantra will choose or create one that they hope to materialize in their own life.

For example, if someone repeats, "I am always at peace, with love in my heart," they likely want to experience peace and love in their life outside of meditation. And hopefully the repetition of this phrase will make this desired experience a reality.

3. Focusing on a body part

I've spent significantly more time with this type of meditation, and it can be quite effective in producing mental clarity.

My girlfriend's sect of Buddhism, in particular, revolves its entire meditation practice around this: practitioners are specifically taught to focus their mind on the center of the belly.

Now if you want to try this type of meditation on your own, you don't need to focus on your belly. Instead, it can be a hand, a foot, neck, leg, etc.

Once you've chosen a body part, pay attention to the feeling, sensations, and aliveness you experience in it. If it aches, let it ache. If it feels soothing, let it be so. Don't get caught up trying to change or resist the feeling; just let it be.

Just like the other practices mentioned above, when you focus on a body part, you're withdrawing attention from your mind. In time this will increase both your feeling of calm and your clarity.

4. Focusing on breathing

If you know anything about meditation, you may be familiar with this kind because it's quite mainstream. Personally I've spent a good six months to a year practicing it, and it is indeed effective.

One of the reasons behind the popularity of breathing meditation is that you can perform it anywhere. You can do it walking around a grocery store, sitting on a couch, or lying on your bed. What's more, it's also incredibly easy to do. All you have to do is simply pay attention to your breathing.

To do this type of meditation, observe your breath (or be fully aware of it) as it moves in and out. You can do this for a few minutes, an hour, or really for as long or short a time as you like. The general idea is that you focus on the breathing process and nothing else.

To make it easier, many people who practice breathing meditation like to count their breaths as they are happening. For example, you breathe in, breathe out, and then count one.

You breathe in, breathe out, then count two.

Keep counting until you reach 5, 10, 20, or whatever number you choose. Then return back to one and start over again.

If you lose track of what number of breath you're on, simply start back at one and try again.

The key to this style of meditation is to not force your breathing. Don't get involved with it, simply watch it instead. Because the breath is one of those unique human functions that can happen either automatically or under our control, it can be a little tricky to do this.

For me personally, when I practiced this form of meditation I always found myself getting too involved in the breathing process - playing around with it and trying to control it. This attempt to control it oftentimes led to more thinking, which is the opposite of what you want during meditation.

With that said, many people don't have this problem and can simply follow their breath as it moves in and out automatically.

What type of meditation do I recommend?

If you have the time and enthusiasm to experiment with the above types of meditation, I encourage you to do so. The "right" type of meditation you should be doing is the one that works for you.

However, through my own experimentation with the various methods mentioned above, I've learned that I'm a big fan of doing absolutely nothing when meditating because it's produced the most results for me. I'll go into more detail about this type of meditation in the next chapter but, before doing so, did you notice a similar theme in the different forms of meditation mentioned above? They all have one characteristic in common...

Withdrawing attention from thought

I mentioned this briefly in the beginning of Chapter 2, and you see it here again in each of the meditation practices described above. Every single form of meditation aims to withdraw attention from mental activity. Instead of focusing on thoughts, you shift your focus to external sounds, your breathing, a mantra, a feeling in the body, etc.

You may ask why this is. As you likely noticed in Chapter 3, the enemy of increased calm, better direction, etc. is too much thinking. By withdrawing attention from mental activity, you bring your attention to the present moment, and everything becomes simpler. Let's try this right now, and see if you can experience it for yourself.

Exercise

This exercise works best if you can do it in a quiet place. If you don't have that option, just try it wherever you're sitting now...

Get comfortable and become completely still. Give your complete attention to the stillness of your body, as well as the feelings and sensations you experience in your arms, legs, hands etc.

Now, begin to pay attention to the sounds you hear as well. Do you hear people talking, wind blowing, birds chirping? Whatever you hear, just notice it - don't criticize it or start thinking about it.

For the next few minutes, continue to give your complete attention to these three things: stillness, bodily sensations, and the sounds around you.

Done yet? Let's go over what just happened

Just like with the different forms of meditation explained above, you withdrew attention from your thoughts, and shifted it to something else: stillness, your body, and sounds. This is all meditation is: shifting attention away from your thought process to your physical experience.

Hopefully, this exercise brought your attention into the present, and gave you a glimpse into the clarity and simplicity that's in store for you with a regular meditation practice.

If you struggled with this exercise, don't worry. I'll go into more depth about the simplest type of meditation I know in the next chapter.

Chapter 5

How ordinary dudes & dudettes can meditate

While I've dabbled in all forms of meditation described in the last chapter, the easiest way I've found to meditate and gain results quickly (and the one I'm going to teach you) is to essentially do nothing.

I know what you're thinking. "You mean I paid for a book to tell me how to do nothing?! I could just do nothing myself!"

Well the truth is, in our fast-paced culture, "nothing" can actually be a bit hard to accomplish. And on top of that, it amazes me how many people I've met who tell me they find it extremely difficult to sit still and feel tormented by non-stop racing thoughts on a daily basis. Neither of these have been problems for me for over a decade. And I feel certain this is a direct result of my meditation practice…

So let's break the ordinary dude and dudettes' simple meditation process down bit by bit, starting with…

Stillness

This is what it all comes down to. I've experimented with so many types of meditation and this has been the most effective thing I've found that links almost all types of meditation (except for maybe walking meditation.)

You have to be still. As I mentioned, many people find it extremely difficult to do this. My response to them is that if you want to make any progress in meditation, you must force yourself to do it.

With that said, don't overwhelm yourself. Take baby steps and be prepared to fail…

An extremely quick (one block paragraph lesson) in failure

Think about it: with any new skill you're trying to acquire, you are going to make some mistakes and fail at first. In fact, failing is quite natural. All of us did it thousands of times when we were children. But for some reason, as adults we've come to believe failure is bad. Yet the people who actually grow to excel at a given skill are the ones who don't give up after not achieving instant success. There's no shame in failure. But if you walk away, you're never going to see what you've been missing – or be able to grow as a human being for that matter.

With this said, you have permission to fail in your meditation practice. Failing is a part of the process, and you will achieve results if you keep trying. Okay, enough of the pep-talk. Here's how you can ease into meditation....

Take baby steps

You have trouble sitting still, and you find the idea of being still 20 minutes downright scary. Okay, no problem.

Day one, sit still for one minute. Then for day two, try two minutes.

Follow this pattern until you hit the five-minute mark. Then practice just sitting still for five minutes, every day for a month. After the first month, bump it up to 10 minutes.

If you're going to notice any results, you want to get up to at least 15 minutes. 20 or 30 is ideal. But we're all busy (even me!), so you just have to do what you can.

If you only have five minutes to meditate some days, do it! Five minutes of meditation is better than none. But the benefits will come quicker the more time you dedicate to it, and the longer your meditation sessions are. The trick is to do it consistently, preferably 5-7 days a week. Some days, it may feel like your meditation isn't doing anything to improve your life. But it is.

Just like a regular exercise routine, there are peaks and valleys in how you experience the results of a regular meditation practice. You'll eventually settle into, and get used to, the daily calm. Once it becomes normal, you may wonder why you need to continue practicing. Keep going, it gets deeper with time. If you quit, the benefits you've gained will reverse to an extent. You'll become more reactive again, and lose some of your calm and clarity. This personally happened to me when my meditation practice nearly fizzled out in my mid 20s.

How do you stay motivated to meditate?

I talk about this more thoroughly in the Conclusion; however, the essential key to staying motivated is to prioritize meditation till it becomes a routine. Obviously, actually developing the routine is the difficult part. So during this adjustment period, you just need to push yourself and prioritize it so that it's one of the top three tasks you must accomplish in your day. Also, think about what you're gaining - increased calm, a better sense of direction in your life, a clearer mind, etc.

If you find yourself thinking about giving up, go back and reread Chapter 3 where I explain the benefits in detail. This is your motivation. And yes, gaining the benefits of regular meditation is absolutely worth it - as they will have a dramatic impact on every other area of your life.

Now let's start meditating, so get comfortable...

No lotus position here! Not even a half lotus. Whether it's through photos on the web or the widely seen image of a monk sitting rigidly, we're constantly inundated with the depiction of people cross-legged on their butts in meditation.

So let me drop a meditation bombshell on you - you don't have to sit. In fact I rarely do so myself.

Contrary to mainstream belief, the position in which you meditate is not that important when it comes to receiving the benefits. Instead, I've found that simply getting into a position where you feel comfortable is far more effective.

Personally, I spent years sitting in the lotus position. Sitting on a cushion with no backrest, I tried to mimic the idea of what I thought meditation was supposed to look like. I did this until one day it finally occurred to me, what's the point?

If you want to do the lotus or half lotus, go right ahead. There's nothing wrong with it. The reason I stopped is because it was distracting to my practice. Instead of concentrating on nothing and just being, my focus was on maintaining a certain position. And my attention was constantly drawn to the pain of attempting to stay in that position – seriously, how many of those monks in meditation look comfortable?

So the main thing is to get comfortable.

This is the half lotus position: one leg rests on top of the other, with one foot (can be either left or right) near the fold of the knee.

Since I'm not flexible enough to manage this, my lovely girlfriend is shown here in the full lotus position: legs are crossed and both feet rest on the thighs.

But there's a catch...straighten your spine!

If you start exploring meditation books, you'll notice that a lot of them advise you to keep your spine straight. It took me a long time to understand why, but there is actually a good reason behind it. Essentially, your posture can have a direct influence on your thoughts and emotions.

If you are slouching during meditation, or feeling pain because your spine is in an awkward position, this is going to prevent you from going deeper into meditation. Essentially, you'll feel distracted by the pain or the uncomfortable feeling. And it will act as a barrier, similar to if there was extremely loud music playing or a lot of activity happening around you while meditating.

Sometimes, you cannot prevent these types of distractions, but whenever feasible it will benefit you to eliminate them as much as possible. This is especially true when you're a beginner and are more easily distracted. At the end of the day, you don't want to stimulate thinking; and feeling pain will generally have that effect.

While I've taken a class on posture and have studied it quite extensively, I'm no expert. So I'm only going to give you some basic guidelines that've worked for me personally.

How to keep your spine straight

I'm including a few pictures here to give you an idea of what a straight spine looks like. Starting with this very handsome ordinary dude himself.

Note, the curve under my back in this photo is exaggerated so you can see it on camera. The actual space between the wall and your back should be a little less than an inch.

Notice in this picture that my spine is not literally straight.

So when I say "straight" spine, we're not talking literal. Instead there should be two curves: one between the base of your spine (at your butt) and your mid back.

The other is between your upper back and head, which creates a space under your neck. See picture below.

Both these curves are natural. But when you try this posture yourself, it may feel a bit strange at first.

Different muscles might feel a bit uncomfortable and tight. And there's a very good reason for this: you likely haven't used them in a long time, due to poor posture.

Try this position yourself

Just like in the full body picture on the last page, the heels of your feet, butt, upper back, and head should be touching the wall.

To prevent your body from being too rigid, slightly bend your knees. Also, make sure to relax your shoulders and let gravity pull them downward to the floor. Many people have a tendency to tighten their shoulders, holding them up and inward.

Once you feel like you're in the right position, maintain this posture for a minute or two.

Try to remember how it feels to be in this position, so that when you meditate you can try and recreate this feeling. Once you've practiced up against the wall a few times, practice straightening your spine during meditation. In fact, make the focus of your first few meditation sessions to get your spine straight.

If after your third or fourth time meditating you still find yourself struggling with posture, and don't feel like your spine is in alignment, don't worry about it. Don't let this prevent you from meditating. Simply do your best and, at the end of the day, just get comfortable.

When meditating, watch - don't resist

Okay, so now you're either sitting comfortably or lying down. Your spine is straight, you're still, you're ready to meditate. Now what?

Well, it's a good idea to set an alarm. That way you can completely focus on stillness and not worry about when you should stop meditating.

After that, pick an object or something to focus on. Since I lie on my back, I stare at a spot on the ceiling like a turned-off light, mark, or scratch. Once you've found your spot, simply be still.

Thoughts are undoubtedly going to pop up in your mind. Just notice them. See what comes up, but don't get caught up in them.

For example, if you suddenly think, "Oh, I was supposed to email Dana earlier today. I need to do that. What should I write in the email? Will she be mad that I didn't email her? I wonder if I should email Mike too?"

Instead, when the thought, "Oh I was supposed to email Dana earlier today" comes up in your mind, just let it go. Don't follow the next thought, "I need to do that", and so on. Your mind likes to think every little thought is the most important thing in the world. 99 times out of 100, it's not.

So just like you would watch a nice-looking car speed by you while waiting at the bus stop, let your thoughts pass by in the same way too. You're not going to chase that nice-looking car when you have a bus to catch (and you probably wouldn't chase it regardless).

So why are you going to chase the nice-looking thought? You have some clarity to gain.

What happens if you really do think of something important?

It happens. Sometimes I think of an awesome idea in meditation or I remember something I need to do that's important. What do I do then?

I make a mental note. I just tell myself to remember this when I'm done with meditation. If more than one important idea pops up, then again I make a mental note of it and think to myself, "I have two things to remember afterward."

I've found that labeling the mental notes with a number is especially helpful. Once I've numbered it, I simply let it go and waste no more time thinking about it. Then when my alarm goes off and I'm finished, the mental notes almost always come back to me.

Now if you're making more than 10 mental notes while meditating, you're doing something wrong. You're overemphasizing the importance of menial things. Seriously, not every thought is important. The majority that pop up are going to be ones you're going to want to let go of immediately, just like that nice-looking car you noticed at the bus stop.

What happens if I can't stop thinking? What if a thought I don't like comes up?

Just like when you're watching car
bus stop, sometimes you're gonn
cars. And sometimes there are going
racing by at once.

It's fine - just let it happen. Everyone has negative
thoughts at one point or another. And racing thoughts
are incredibly common. It's just how the mind works.
So instead of fighting your thoughts, let them pass
and do your best not to get caught up in them.

But if you do end up following a chain of thoughts,
don't worry about it. Simply try again and keep
practicing. The roadway of your mind isn't always
going to be clogged with cars - I promise.

The truth is, nothing lasts forever. So just keep
practicing, and keep being still, and those unwanted
and racing thoughts will disappear on their own.

Thoughts aren't the only things to notice

When you're still, you're not just gonna notice
thoughts. You're also gonna notice sounds,
sensations in your body, and maybe smells.

Just like with thoughts, let them pass. No need to
start thinking about them. Just notice them. So if you

r some annoying dog that won't shut up (a
ommon problem for me in Thailand), just let it go.
There's no need to waste time getting upset or
thinking about it. The sound will pass effortlessly by
itself.

Your goal during the meditation practice is to be still,
and not get caught up in thinking. Although it may not
seem like it at first, in time meditation can actually be
very relaxing.

Stillness is enough

After you're still, you actually don't have to do
anything else. Seriously, just be still. If you do this at
least five days a week for 15-30 minutes, this little
change will make a dramatic difference in your life,
your mental clarity, and your general disposition.

What if I can't stop my racing thoughts? What if it's not working?!

Even I have bad days in meditation, and I'm sure they
happen to almost all people who practice. Perfect
meditation sessions don't happen every day.

But when you're just starting out, a couple bad days in a row can make you feel like you're doing something wrong - and that it's not working. Maybe you think it's time to give up.

Don't. Just go back to the basics. Straighten your spine (if you can), get comfortable, be still. This is making a difference no matter what your thoughts might tell you.

Even if you do get caught up in the racing thoughts, just bring your attention back to the stillness of your body. Keep at it and I assure you that you'll start seeing some positive changes in your life.

How does this ordinary dude meditate?

Let me show you. I lie down on my bed and bend my legs so that my spine remains in alignment. It's important not to lie flat on your back with your legs straight out like this.

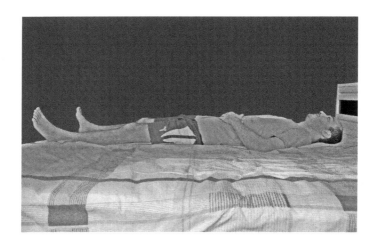

Your spine may seem straight, but it's not. You're actually putting undue pressure on your spine.

Keep your legs bent instead, like in the picture below.

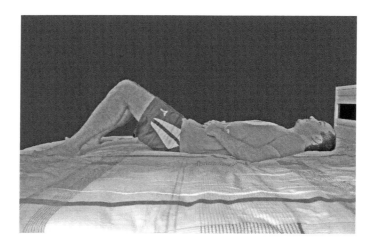

How bent will vary from person to person, so just experiment until you find an angle that is comfortable for you.

As you'll notice from the picture, when I lie on my back, I don't place a pillow under my head. I just keep my legs bent and lie flat on the bed.

In fact, a pillow is not necessarily a good idea, unless it is thin. With a thicker pillow, you're going to be bending your head too far forward. This throws your spine out of alignment, putting it in an awkward position. If you want some support under your neck, try a folded towel or a thin pillow like I mentioned above. Personally though, I prefer my head resting on the bed.

Like I mentioned earlier, I set a timer before I get started. Then it's all about lying back, finding my spot on the ceiling, and focusing on stillness.

Any other ways to meditate that don't involve lying down?

While I rarely meditate this way any more, you can also meditate comfortably by sitting in a chair. Simply find a sturdy chair, with no wheels, and have yourself a seat.

Just like lying down, you should try to straighten your spine as much as possible. So first off, make sure you're not slouching and sitting on your tailbone like the photo below.

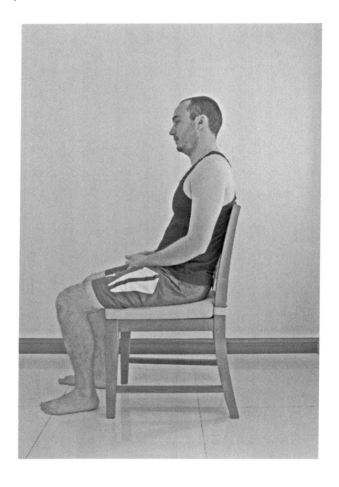

In the previous photo, notice how my shoulders are slumped forward and that the curve in my lower back is missing. This is the type of sitting position you want to avoid. Instead, you want to make sure your lower back is slightly arched like this.

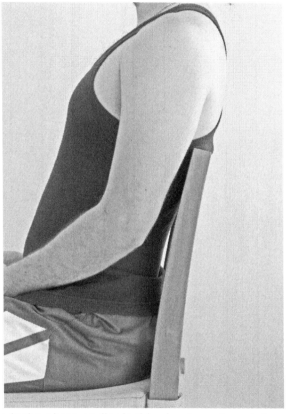

Just like in the photo earlier in this chapter, where I demonstrate the two spinal curves, this curve is also exaggerated so it appears on camera. The distance between your back and the chair should be between 0.5 – 1 inch.

Next, keep your feet flat on the floor. And then simply relax your shoulders, letting them hang loose. Your posture should look something like the one I demonstrate below.

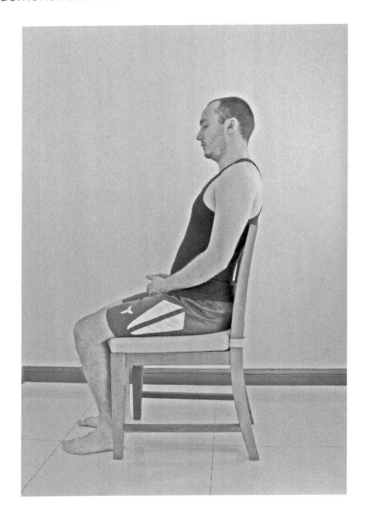

Now remember, if you struggle with this posture, it is not an excuse to avoid meditation. The same rule applies to this as in the lying down position, or any other position you may try: get comfortable. Once you're as comfortable as possible, find a spot to focus on or close your eyes, and be still.

Of course, if you want to try other positions, like the lotus or half lotus for example, you absolutely can. The position is secondary to the act of stillness. So whether you sit, lie, kneel or whatever, all you need to remember is to focus on being still, and that's it. Do this for at least 15 minutes a day, five days a week, and it will make a difference - I guarantee it.

Exercise

To take this a step further, I want to guide you through an exercise that is very effective for putting the endless stream of racing thoughts in perspective.

Stop what you're doing right now. Become very still, and just sit wherever you are and pay attention to your thoughts.

Is there a thought in your mind? If so, observe it. What happens to it? Whether it's good or bad, don't resist it or continue thinking about it - just watch and see what happens. You'll notice that it eventually disappears.

Sit still for a minute or two longer and continue to watch your thoughts. You'll probably notice that thoughts come and go, just like the clouds in the sky.

I challenge you to try this exercise once a day, every day for the next week. Find a few minutes to slow down, become still, and simply observe your thoughts. If you do this, you'll see just how impermanent your thoughts actually are. There is no need to treat 99% of them like an emergency.

Chapter 6

Getting started - 10 beginner questions answered

1. Why is meditation so effective? Is there any science behind it?

Meditation literally changes the way your brain functions. The region of the brain known as the Default Mode Network, or DMN, which is responsible for wandering and self-centered thoughts when you're not actively thinking, decreases in activity with regular meditation practice.

Additionally, meditation increases the thickness of the cortical region of the brain (the area responsible for learning and memory) and can shrink the amygdala (the part of the brain responsible for "fight or flight"). The results of these changes provide increased emotional stability, concentration, and ability to learn.

As for research to actually back these claims up, there have been tons of studies done on the science behind meditation, including by reputable institutions such as *UCLA and *Harvard.

In addition to these resources, a simple Google search of "how meditation changes the brain" or "science behind meditation" will bring up loads of other results for further reading if you are so inclined.

*For those interested in the studies I'm referring to, you can find them below:
- Harvard Study: Google "8 weeks to a better brain" or type in this link: http://news.harvard.edu/gazette/story/2011/01/eight-weeks-to-a-better-brain/
- UCLA Study: Google "forever younger meditation" or type this link: http://journal.frontiersin.org/article/10.3389/fpsyg.2014.01551/full

2. What type of environment is right for meditation? Is total silence important?

Generally, a quiet and comfortable environment is best for meditation. A quiet room in your house, where you won't be disturbed, works well. This is especially important for beginners, as the more noise and chaos you have going on around you, the harder it will be to stay still and withdraw attention from thinking.

While I prefer dim lights myself, light is really not a factor that enhances or diminishes meditation. Bear in mind, though, that if you meditate with the lights off, there's a greater chance of you falling asleep.

As for music...it's best to avoid your Top 40 and most types of music you hear on the radio. When you listen to anything with a lot of dialogue or lyrics, you may start thinking about what's being said or even sing along if it happens to be a song.

So if you want to experiment with noise, it's okay to do so. Just try nature sounds or some soft music with little or no dialogue.

3. What time of day should I meditate?

There is no right or wrong time of day to meditate. But if you're unsure of when to do it, just try a certain time of day that you think you'll like: maybe before bed, during your lunch break, or first thing in the morning.

Now, for those who have difficulty sticking to a regular 5-7 days a week meditation practice, there are two times that I've found to be most effective for developing a routine.

The first is immediately once you get home from work (or if you work at home, as soon as you're done for the day). When I was following this schedule, I was able to easily maintain a 5 days a week routine.

However, when I started trying to shift this into an everyday routine, I encountered a problem.

Usually once or twice during the week (especially Fridays) something would come up and I'd go straight from work to another activity. Sometimes I wouldn't get home till after midnight (and be sleepy) and sometimes I would be drunk.

As you've probably guessed, neither of these scenarios are optimal for meditation, or for your motivation. So I moved my meditation to a time where it's virtually impossible to miss it – first thing in the morning.

Now, the first thing I do when I wake up is meditate. Since I've made the switch, the only time I've missed it is when I'm on vacation. That's not to say I won't in the future (I probably will if I have to get up at 4am for something). But it is incredibly easy to stick with this time of day.

You get it out of the way first thing in the morning, and then there's no chance that any surprises in your schedule cause you to miss it.

4. What should I wear? What should I do with my hands?

It all comes down to what feels comfortable. Wear comfortable clothes and put your hands in a position that feels comfortable. When I meditate I wear anything from just boxers, to shorts and a t-shirt, or some loose-fitting pajama pants. As for the hands, I usually rest them gently on my belly like in the picture below:

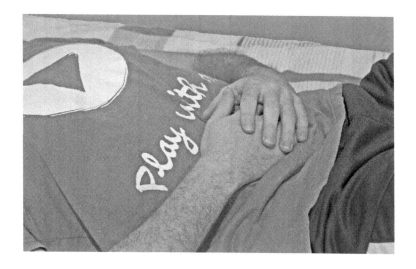

When I sit, I'll rest them on my lap, palms up like in the following photo.

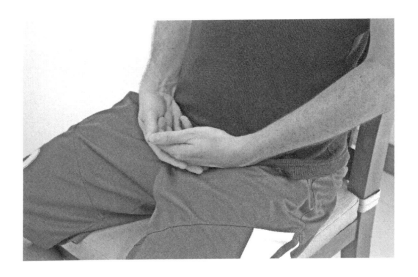

As with so much else written in this book, comfortability is key. Don't let the point of your meditation practice to become holding your body in a rigid position, wearing a specific outfit, or acting a certain way. Be yourself, and remember stillness is king.

5. What should I expect my first time meditating?

I wish I could share my own experience here. But as it's been over a decade since I've started, I don't really remember it too well. However, after talking with first-time meditators, and from my own experience returning to meditation on multiple occasions over the years, I can tell you this. It's going to be difficult to sit still. And you're probably going to feel uncomfortable with some of the feelings that pop up.

So what do you do? You meditate anyway. Like I mentioned earlier in the book, take small steps. If it's incredibly difficult, just do a minute for your first session. And then work your way up to five, ten and so on.

If you want to just dive in and do a longer meditation session at the get-go, I completely encourage you to do so. Every time I've returned to meditation, I've just bitten the bullet and gone right back to 20 minutes. Perhaps this is because I know what to expect though...I'm fairly certain the first time I meditated it was for less than 10 minutes.

6. It is insanely difficult to sit still - any pointers?

When you first start meditating, sitting still can feel like the equivalent of someone slowly inching a finger towards your eye, with you being forced to keep it open. In other words, it can be excruciating, especially if you have a lot of built-up anxiety or racing thoughts.

To counter this, try bringing your attention to the feeling in your hands or feet, or listen to the sounds around you, like the wind, rain, air conditioner, footsteps or whatever. This will take your attention off the overwhelming emotion you may be experiencing and help you relax.

One exception though - avoid listening to conversations. When you listen to people talk, you're more likely to start thinking about what's being said, which is not what we're trying to do here.

7. I have an itch. My nose is running. I really have to use the toilet now! Can I relieve myself?

When it comes to an itch or a slight runny nose, try to remain still and let it be. Yes, it can be difficult to do this, but the key to a successful meditation session is stillness.

So instead of scratching the itch or wiping your nose, just experience the sensation. No it doesn't sound fun, and you'll initially be inclined to take action and relieve it. But usually within what feels like 20 to 30 seconds (on rare occasions it can last a few minutes), the sensation will no longer bother you and will likely go away on its own.

Of course, if you're dreadfully sick and there's snot oozing out of your nose at a rapid pace, then yes, it may make sense to wipe it. And if you have a terrible case of diarrhea, then absolutely go and relieve yourself in the toilet. There are exceptions!

So have I personally ever scratched an itch or wiped my nose during meditation? Of course. But it's on a very rare occasion. 99% of the time I just ignore it, and it goes away by itself.

8. I keep falling asleep when I'm meditating. What should I do?

One of the reasons some teachers advise against meditation lying down is because some people have a tendency to fall asleep. This can be especially easy for those who meditate first thing in the morning.

If that's you, one trick to avoid this is to take a shower before you meditate. That should help wake you up a bit, so you don't feel like your meditation is just an excuse to catch some more zzz's. Now, if you're meditating later in the day and still have trouble staying awake, another idea is to simply try sitting meditation.

And of course, if you've been meditating this whole time with your eyes closed and wonder why you keep falling asleep, then all you have to do is make one simple adjustment: meditate with your eyes open.

9. Is it okay to eat or drink before I meditate?

It depends on what. Water is always okay. Although, best not to chug a lot and have to pee during your meditation! However, I was always taught to avoid food, and all beverages besides water, within an hour of meditation. And this is something that I try to stick with to this day.

Just like how some noises can stimulate thinking, foods and liquids (besides water) will stimulate your body. And the goal of meditation is to experience the least amount of stimulation as possible while remaining still.

10. Should I take a meditation class or find a teacher?

I always tell people meditation is the easy part. Forming the habit is what most dudes struggle with.

For this reason, one of the biggest benefits of having a teacher is they can help you form the habit - as well as answer questions, and introduce you to different styles of meditation and other aspects of the practice.

For those who would rather forgo the teacher, I encourage you to check out the follow up to this book, *An Ordinary Dude's Guide to Habit*. This book was written specifically to help you form and break common habits, such as quitting smoking, exercising weekly and, of course, meditating daily.

If you choose to go it alone, you may want to try the exceptional Headspace app (discussed more in the Further Reading section of this book). Regardless of how you proceed, remember the key is to be still.

Conclusion

Developing your own practice - meditation is like flossing your teeth

Seriously...flossing, just like meditation, is great for your health. I've been a regular flosser since I was 18. Why 18 you ask? Well, basically, I was heading off to college, and my parents were no longer footing my dental bills. I knew that if I wanted to avoid expensive trips to the dentist's office, I needed to floss my teeth. To this day, I've still never had a cavity (I'm 33). Even better, my dentists are always complimenting me on how well I take care of my teeth.

So, the thing about flossing your teeth is that it's a real pain in the ass. Before I started doing it regularly, my dentist would always complain about me not flossing enough. But with my parents paying for all my trips to the dentist, I just didn't care. And truthfully, I was lazy and didn't want to put in the effort.

What changed was that I made it a priority to floss every day (I actually think I started flossing 5 days a week, and then worked my way up to 7). In college I knew I wasn't going to have a lot of money, and I couldn't afford costly dental appointments - especially when I could be spending that money on beer, which was extremely important to me at that time. This was enough motivation for me to floss consistently.

So what about meditation? How can you make it a priority?

The thing is, if you've never meditated, you don't know what you're missing out on. You haven't experienced the benefits of having smoother relationships, more lightheartedness, less emotional turmoil, more calmness and patience, and more clarity - all things that it brings into your life.

You may be so used to the day-to-day turmoil that you have no motivation to change. When I didn't floss in high school, I had no reason to start. But when I saw the potential consequences of not changing (when I went off to college), I had to do something.

The same was true when I started meditation at 19. I saw my anxiety getting worse, my personal relationships suffering, and felt a growing sense of isolation.

The point is that if your life isn't getting better, don't wait till it's falling apart to make a change. Meditation is one way you can create a positive difference now.

So if you want to stay motivated to meditate, always think back to the benefits. Think about the daily calm, clarity, and sense of direction you'll gain from a consistent meditation practice.

After a month or two of regular practice, your stress levels will decrease. You'll start to notice you're less bothered by the daily annoyances that once irritated you.

After six months or a year, your calm will start to take root. Just like a sapling grows into a towering tree, your sense of peace will become more difficult to shake. Yes, you will hit plateaus where it feels like nothing is changing.

Keep going.

Just like physical exercise for your body, just like flossing your teeth on a regular basis, you are gaining benefits whether you see them or not.

Final thoughts

This book is about the simplest way of meditation I know: one that any ordinary dude or dudette can pick up quickly, that's not overwhelming or "out there", and that has been truly beneficial to me.

If you are curious to explore different types of meditation practices, I encourage you to do so. What it comes down to is you need to find what's right for you.

However, if you're perfectly happy with the method I've shared with you in this book, know that it is enough to make a world of difference.

Of course, though, meditation isn't going to miraculously solve all your problems. Yes, you will still get stressed from time to time, and encounter difficulties, as even I still do. But when I look back at where I was before I started meditating, my life is now 10 times better. For me, it has been the key to a happier, more centered life, filled with more peace and clarity. And it can do the same for you too.

However you choose to meditate, don't be afraid to try something new, or even to fail.

To this day, I still experiment with my own practice from time to time. The goal, however, is always the same: clarity, calmness, and more peace.

Whatever form of meditation is going to increase this for you, that is the one you should be doing.

Have questions about your meditation practice? Passing through Bangkok and want to grab a beer? Feel free to get in touch, and drop me a line at john@ordinarydudemeditation.com.

Further Reading

As suggested by an Amazon reviewer, I felt it was a good idea to include some resources I found incredibly helpful when I first started meditating.

Many of the books listed below are not specifically about meditation and, as I encountered most of them in my new-age hippy phase discussed in Chapter 2, many fall under the Buddhist and Spiritual categories.

With that said, many of these books helped shape my outlook and contributed significantly to the style of meditation I teach in this book.

Headspace (the app), by Andy Puddicombe
Though not a book, it seems appropriate to start this list with a legit meditation resource. Headspace is awesome. A portion of my in-person/video teaching lessons are heavily influenced by Headspace. Andy Puddicombe knows what he's talking about, and if you're looking for guided meditation, you can't go wrong here.

The Power of Now, by Eckhart Tolle
When I was becoming frustrated with breathing meditation (mentioned in Chapter 4) and searching for a new style, I just happened to come across

Eckhart Tolle's *Power of Now*. This and Eckhart's other books have a heavy influence on the style of meditation I teach in this book, specifically his philosophies on stillness and focusing your attention on body parts.

Stillness Speaks, by Eckhart Tolle
Another great Eckhart read, but not as heavy and heady as *Power of Now*. This is an excellent book to pick up when you have a few minutes of quiet time.

The Miracle of Mindfulness, by Thich Nhat Hanh
When I was first beginning meditation 15 years ago, this book was extremely helpful to me. There are practical, helpful teachings on breathing meditation and how to incorporate mindfulness into daily tasks - such as washing the dishes, walking, doing the laundry, and more.

The Tao of Pooh, by Benjamin Hoff
Like Buddhism, Taoism has had a big influence on my views, and this book couldn't be a better introduction. It provides a very simple, easy-to-understand, fun introduction to Taoism and its philosophical ideas. One of my all-time favorite books.

The Way of Zen, by Alan Watts

Many of my readers are Alan Watts fan. It's no surprise. My philosophies are heavily influenced by him. This book, in particular, was incredibly interesting to me when I was first studying Buddhism and practicing meditation. There's a lot of info about the history of this religion, as well as Taoism and Zen.

The Book: on the Taboo Against Knowing Who You Are, by Alan Watts

In my younger years, when I was soul searching and looking for answers about the truth of existence, the self and who I really was, this book was extremely helpful to me. Recommended for those interested in enlightenment.

Wherever You Go, There You Are, by Jon Kabat-Zinn

An exceptional read on meditation and mindfulness. While *An Ordinary Dude's Guide to Meditation* is a simple, straightforward and very focused guide, *Wherever You Go, There You Are* offers a broader perspective - getting into practices like walking meditation, parenting as meditation and more. Would be a great follow up read to ODGM.

Shining in Plain View, by John Wheeler

Wheeler, who I talk extensively about in my upcoming book *An Ordinary Dude's Guide to Enlightenment*, had a profound effect on my outlook. It is in fact John Wheeler's books that knocked me out of my new-age hippy phase, and is probably my favorite book on list for this very reason. **Tip:** I think this book is currently out of print. You can get used copies on Amazon, but they are expensive. I'd recommend searching for this one at your library, as well as checking out any John Wheeler books you can get your hands on.

Zen Stories of the Samurai, by Neal Dunnigan

Ancient Japanese stories of cool Zen masters and samurais, imparting little nuggets of wisdom along the way. Like *Stillness Speaks*, this is a great book to pick up and read when you have a few minutes of quiet. The illustrations are a nice touch as well.

The Art of Intermittent Fasting, by Connor Thompson

I first came across intermittent fasting during a very strange month in my life. My doctor was raving about it, some monks I was talking to at my girlfriend's temple were telling me about it, and then my author buddy Connor Thompson released this book. I find intermittent fasting to compliment meditation well and have a lot of excellent health benefits (supposedly preventing cancer being one of them), and this book in particular is a great beginner guide that I love. I may one day add an intermittent fasting guide to the Ordinary Dude Series, but until then, I'd recommend this one.

Solve for Happy, by Mo Gawdat

I came across this book by accident. And I was blown away by its unique approach to discovering happiness. The author is an engineer, so he uses this background to show readers how they can "engineer" happiness for themselves. I found this approach both refreshing and practical, as the book explains that happiness is our natural state. We just need to find out where we lost our way, much like how an engineer searches for the breaking point when a machine stops functioning correctly.

Also by the author

The legit sequel to this book, *An Ordinary Dude's Guide to Habit* was written to help dudes with the most difficult part of meditation – forming the habit. That said, this guide covers more than meditation and teaches 23 tactics to help you change any habit.

A Dude's Guide to the Couch is a spin-off of Ordinary Dude Guides. There's pizza. There's beer. There's naps. And also 70 amazing things you can do on your couch, references to dude icons (Lebowski, Bill & Ted, Chuck Norris, and more), and lots of "adult" cartoons. No it's not what you're thinking. This isn't an X-rated guide, but it's certainly not for children. Mostly for entertainment purposes and laughs.

Available at Amazon.com

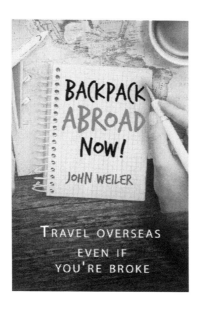

Dream of vagabonding the globe for months on end? Imagine the freedom. The adventure. The new experiences that will forever change your life. But first...how do you get abroad?

Backpack Abroad Now! will teach you how to plan your adventure, **one step at a time**. I saved up for an epic 11-month backpacking journey, while earning less than $17,000 a year, and have been living and traveling abroad for over 6 years and counting. This is the guide I wish I had before starting...when I was overwhelmed and broke, dreaming about traveling the world.

Available at Amazon.com

Special Thanks

While I certainly could have written this book without any second opinion, the quality would not be nearly as high without the help of my friends and family who gave early feedback.

So thank you to Andy Hasdal, Nick Zeleznak, Maria Wardian, Paco Ramirez, Chelsea Mulvey Wolfe, and Julie Weiler. Also, thank you to my editors Chris Wotton and Eve Jones. And a very special shout out to Ivan Diaz and Kris Kristensen. Your comments about adding more metaphors and examples made a huge difference in the final content of the book.

I'd also like to thank my lovely girlfriend Arissara Suratanon for taking the beautiful, high quality pictures, and also for putting up with all the long-hours and weekends it took me to get this done. I couldn't have made this without your support.

Happy to have you all in my life, and I'm so thankful that you were willing to carve out some time in your busy schedules to give this a read. This final version of the book wouldn't have been possible without you.

And to every dude who's left an Amazon review

Thank **YOU**

An Ordinary Dude's Guide to Meditation has thus far been a huge success for me. Thousands of copies have been sold and the book has been an Amazon #1 best seller on multiple occasions. With that said, this success would not be possible without all the reviews left by friends, fans and complete strangers.

So to each of you, I want to personally thank every dude that has left a review at the time of this writing. From the one star to five star reviews this book has received, and everything in between, I am appreciative of you taking your valuable time to share your thoughts.

So without further ado, thank you to the following folks:

Gareth, Study Shortcuts and Exam Tips from Oxford Grads, bkkbob, HurleyCub, John H, Samantha, Steve Olson, Cape, Bill, Phil H, Robin, Ivan Dimanov, RHM, Katherine Gaylord, Kevin M Carolan, Bruce Miles, Oneson, Chantaine Bulluck, GrumpyOldMan, Gusto, FJ1200, Brian D, Kongpop Wiriya-Akaradecha, Susan Burke, ProfRedSweater, K.

Kristensen, MWolfe, g b, meghan, Rob Y, Andrew Hasdal, Houston Mike, Albert, theeddyadams, Travis Bennett, Corby Stallman, Adam L. Selley, TJ, Deb, Kenneth, Scott Pressimone, Dee Arr, Linda, MrsBakon, Kris Woo, Mrs GA Morris, John Rogerson, Michael M. King Hippo, Jennifer N., vincon, Nick Zeleznak, and S. Domanski.

About The Author

John Weiler is a writer, former television producer and scriptwriter, and ordinary dude who has now lived in Bangkok, Thailand, for 5 years. He currently works at a marketing company as a writer, content director, and project director four days a week, and then spends the rest of his time creating new content for Ordinary Dude Meditation, and attempting to keep in touch with his fellow dudes via his mailing list at www.ordinarydudemeditation.com

As the book suggests, John is a hardcore meditator. And as of this writing, he has now been meditating for 15 years, and has spent the past four years meditating every day for 20 minutes. In his free time, John likes to travel to, and explore the cultures of Asian countries with his dudette. He's also an avid NBA hoops fan, lover of all things coffee and beer, and enjoys grilling with his buddies whenever he can.

Printed in Great Britain
by Amazon